Close to the Wild
Siberian Tigers in a Zoo

Close to the Wild
Siberian Tigers in a Zoo

by Thomas Cajacob and Teresa Burton

photographs by Thomas Cajacob

A Carolrhoda Nature Watch Book

Carolrhoda Books, Inc./Minneapolis

For Joey, Bobby, Johnny, and Laura

The authors wish to thank the Minnesota Zoo for its cooperation and for its dedication to life and care of the wild.
Special thanks to Dr. U.S. Seal for his great gift of knowledge.

Text copyright © 1986 Thomas Cajacob and Teresa Burton
Illustrations © 1986 Thomas Cajacob

Manufactured in the United States of America

This book is available in two editions:
Library binding by Carolrhoda Books, Inc.
Soft cover by First Avenue Editions
241 First Avenue North
Minneapolis, Minnesota 55401

Library of Congress Cataloging in Publication Data

Cajacob, Thomas.
  Close to the wild.

  Summary: A behind-the-scenes look at Siberian tigers living in a major natural-habitat zoo focusing on various aspects of tiger behavior, the care provided by the zoo, and the zoo's role in preserving endangered species.
  1. Tigers—Juvenile literature. 2. Zoo animals—Juvenile literature. [1. Tigers. 2. Zoo animals. 3. Zoos] I. Burton, Teresa. II. Title. III. Title: Siberian tigers in a zoo.
  QL737.C23C34 1986   636.974428   84-29299
  ISBN 0-87614-227-7 (lib. bdg.)
  ISBN 0-87614-451-2 (pbk.)

2 3 4 5 6 7 8 9 10 95 94 93 92 91 90 89 88 87 86

Of the big cats—lions, tigers, leopards, jaguars, and cheetahs—tigers are the biggest, and the Siberian tiger is the biggest of all. A full-grown male can weigh as much as 600 pounds (270 kg), though 400 pounds (180 kg) is the average, and measure over 13 feet from its head to the tip of its tail. Females tend to be smaller and usually weigh under 300 pounds (135 kg).

Because their homes, or **habitats**, are in cold climates where temperatures can drop to -40 degrees F (-40 degrees C), Siberians have adapted to cold-weather living. In the winter their coats are longer and thicker than those of other tigers, and the layer of fat beneath their coats can be two inches thick. Their paler coloring provides them with camouflage suited to their habitat.

A century ago, tigers roamed by the thousands throughout much of Asia. Today they survive in only parts of that range. Siberians can still be found on the mountain slopes or in the forests of northern China, parts of Siberia, and North Korea, but scientists estimate that only several hundred of them exist in the wild today.

Tigers are generally more active at night than during the day. We say that they are **nocturnal**. During the day, a tiger usually rests. At dusk, it begins to hunt for food.

Siberian tigers prey on deer, elk, wild boars, bears, wolves, badgers, foxes, and sometimes salmon, but the hungrier the tiger, the less picky it becomes, sometimes satisfying its hunger with rodents. A few old or sickly tigers have become aggressive, but there is no known instance of a Siberian eating a human being. Generally tigers avoid people.

Tigers have keen eyesight and hearing, but they cannot run long distances. A tiger hunts by stalking until it is within 15 to 20 yards of its prey, then charging. It will chase its prey for only about 200 yards before giving up and only catches what it's after about 20 to 30% of the time. Since a Siberian tiger needs to eat about 300 pounds of meat each month, hunting takes up a great deal of its time.

A Siberian tiger kills its captured prey by biting it on the back of the neck with its sharp fangs. It then drags the prey to a sheltered place, such as a downed tree or nearby lair. The tiger might stay with its kill for several days, feeding, grooming itself, and resting until it has eaten most of the meat and

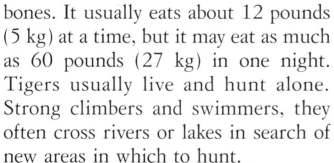

bones. It usually eats about 12 pounds (5 kg) at a time, but it may eat as much as 60 pounds (27 kg) in one night. Tigers usually live and hunt alone. Strong climbers and swimmers, they often cross rivers or lakes in search of new areas in which to hunt.

Natural Habitats of World Tiger Population

■ range of Siberians
▢ range of other tigers

At one time, Siberian tigers ranged over much of China, Korea, and Siberia, but due to expanding human populations, the Siberian's habitat has decreased dramatically. People have cut down forests formerly inhabited by the tigers and planted crops in their place. They have hunted the Siberian's prey, and they have sometimes hunted the tigers as well.

With the takeover of so much of its habitat, the Siberian tiger population has rapidly decreased. Scientists estimate that in 1960 there were 250 Siberians in the wild. By 1981 the Siberian

tiger population had decreased to between 35 and 70 in North Korea and 75 to 100 in northern China. Because Soviet authorities established **reserves** to protect their Siberian tigers, in 1981 the Soviet Union had from 150 to 300 tigers. These reserves have not been totally effective, however, since tigers often roam far beyond the boundaries of the reserves.

When all the animals of one kind, or **species**, die, that species becomes **extinct**. Siberian tigers are in danger of extinction. They have been classified as an **endangered species**.

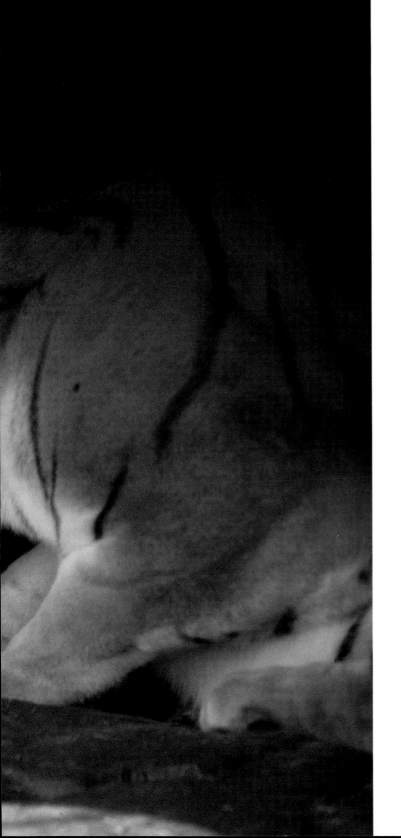

Helping to save endangered species is one of the zoo's most important jobs, and zoos all over the world have become involved in efforts to save the Siberian tiger. Although the United States and the Soviet Union disagree politically on many things, they work together to save the Siberian.

When a zoo decides to get a new Siberian, it's not just a simple matter of picking out a handsome tiger or taking whatever tiger is available. The choice of which tiger to take is much more complicated.

Every living thing inherits traits from its ancestors. You inherited things that everyone can see, such as the color of your eyes and skin, your height, or the shape of your nose. You also inherited things that cannot be seen. You may have inherited some allergies, for instance, or a tendency to get stomachaches, or a gift for music. Taken together, the traits that you inherited are called your **genetic makeup**, and your genetic makeup is different from that of any other living thing.

13

You inherited your genetic makeup from your mother and father. If you have brothers and sisters, they also inherited their genetic makeups from your parents. Your genetic makeup is unique to you, but you are much more genetically simi-lar to a brother or sister than you are to other people.

In order for a species to survive and remain strong, it is important that babies be born to parents of different genetic makeups, not to parents as closely related

as you are to your brother or sister. This is important for people, and it is important for tigers as well.

When a zoo "goes shopping" for a Siberian tiger, it looks closely at the tiger's genetic makeup. The zoo wants to find a strong, healthy tiger. It also wants a tiger genetically different from the tigers it already has. The zoo hopes that its tigers will mate and have cubs. It wants the parents of those cubs to come from different genetic backgrounds.

Most Siberian tigers in the U.S. come from the U.S.S.R. We don't buy these tigers—they are gifts. Nevertheless, getting a tiger from the Soviet Union to the United States is expensive.

Once a tiger that meets a zoo's needs has been found, a representative from the zoo travels to the Soviet Union to pick it up. The zoo representative will be responsible for the tiger throughout the journey.

First the animal is given a shot of a **sedative**. The sedative puts the tiger to sleep. This shot is followed with shots of the **vaccines** that are required before the tiger will be allowed into the United States. Finally the tiger is loaded into a travel crate and put aboard a plane. No other drugs will be given to it for the rest of its journey.

The flight from Moscow, where many tigers are picked up, to New York City

lasts about 10 to 12 hours. By the time the plane has landed, the sedative has worn off, and the tiger is restless and hot. If New York is not the final destination, the zoo representative will cool down the tiger by spraying it with a hose before continuing the journey.

Recently two Siberian tigers were being shipped out of the Soviet Union at the same time. One was headed for Canada and the other for the United States, but the crates got mixed up and the tigers wound up at the wrong destinations. This was not a big problem, however. The zoos involved had already made plans for their tigers to travel to other zoos as part of a special breeding program, so eventually they wound up where they were supposed to be.

These photos show how a Siberian is prepared for shipment overseas. This tiger is being flown to China.

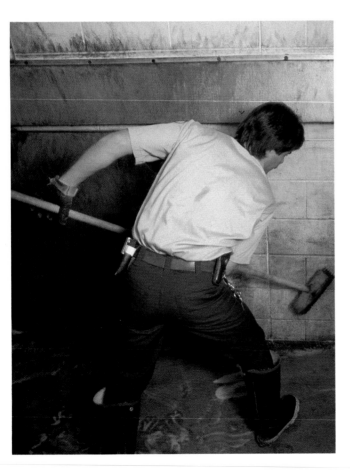

When the tiger arrives at its new home, it is put in **isolation**, or kept separate from the other tigers at the zoo, for three weeks. The isolation area is 10 feet by 10 feet with a concrete floor and steel bars on one side. There is also an outdoor holding area that is 10 feet

high and 15 feet long with steel bars for walls.

While in the isolation quarters, the **keeper** who will be caring for this tiger gets to know a little about its temperament and sees how it reacts to people in general. The keeper will play an impor- tant role in the tiger's new life, supplying the tiger with its daily food, water, and vitamin needs and keeping its living quarters clean. The keeper also maintains a close watch on the tiger and is often the first to notice if a tiger seems sick or behaves strangely.

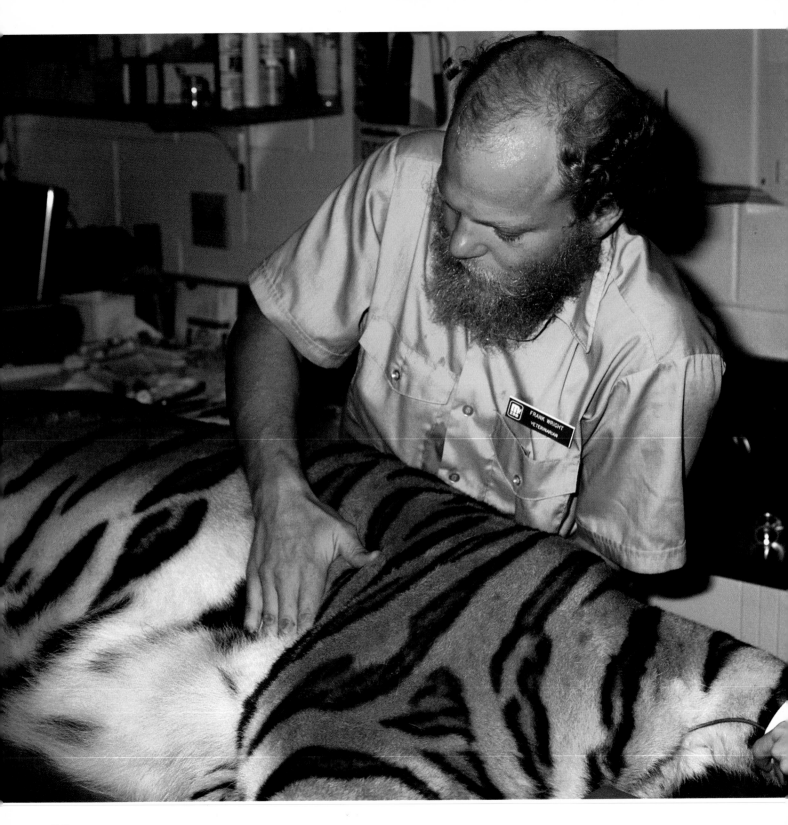

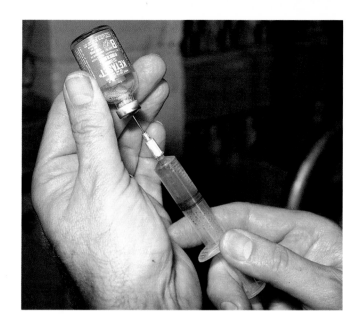

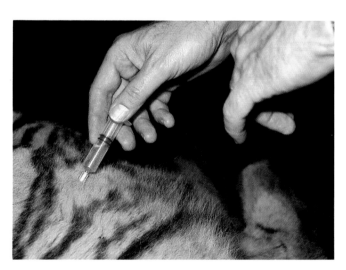

During the isolation period, the tiger gets a complete medical examination by the zoo **veterinarian**. The veterinarian wants to make absolutely certain that the tiger is healthy and that it will be able to adapt to its new environment.

After the isolation period is over, the tiger is moved to the tiger barn, which is the holding area for the tigers. The holding area is located close to the actual tiger exhibit area.

While in the holding area, the tiger is taught "shifting." Shifting is moving from one cage to another as cage doors are opened. Shifting is done when cages need cleaning.

In some ways a Siberian tiger's life in a natural-habitat zoo is similar to its life in the wild. Both in the wild and in captivity, tigers mark their **territories** by spraying urine along the boundaries and by scratching their claws and rubbing their cheeks against boundary trees. In the wild, a male's territory usually includes an area that overlaps with two or three females' territories. The male will mate with these females.

In the zoo, a male and a female tiger may be placed together for mating, and mother tigers are put together with their cubs. But in general tigers—male and female alike—do not get along particularly well, whether in the zoo or in the wild. For this reason, zoo tigers are usually kept separated while on exhibit.

The Siberian tiger area varies in size from zoo to zoo. In the zoo pictured here, it is 3 acres (1.2 hectares). This allows room to show two groups of tigers. One group may consist of a mother with her cubs while the other group might be a male and a female who are together for breeding. The groups are divided by a 20-foot-high chain-link fence that runs the length of the area.

No tiger likes heat, and, both in the wild and at the zoo, tigers spend a good part of their days resting in the shade or lying in a quiet pool of water to cool off. At night, however, the life of a zoo tiger is very different from the life of a wild tiger. At dusk, a wild tiger begins to hunt for food. Zoo tigers are fed a prepared diet, called Feline Ration, consisting of horse meat and vitamins. A large cat may eat as much as 10 pounds (4.5 kg) of Feline Ration a day, thus eliminating its need to hunt.

The zoo tiger's nighttime hunting instinct is also changed by the fact that they are brought inside at night. The instinct to hunt is then replaced by the desire to sleep. Even though the zoo tiger's night habits change, they still spend their days much like wild tigers do—pacing, playing, and taking the ever-famous "cat naps."

At a natural-habitat zoo, every attempt is made to recreate as closely as possible an animal's environment in the wild. In the case of Siberian tigers, the habitat consists of rocky terrain, a creek or small pond, and a large grassy, wooded area. Of course, a Siberian's zoo home is likely to be in a climate much warmer than its home in the wild, but the Siberians don't seem to be too bothered by this.

Sometimes during the routine care of a tiger, a keeper may notice a change in the Siberian's behavior, such as loss of appetite or listlessness, or a physical symptom such as loss of fur. Then the zoo vet is called in to do an examination.

The exam usually includes taking blood and urine samples to check for disorders such as vitamin deficiency. If a specific problem is noticed, the vet will make a more local exam and carefully check the part of the tiger that seems to be

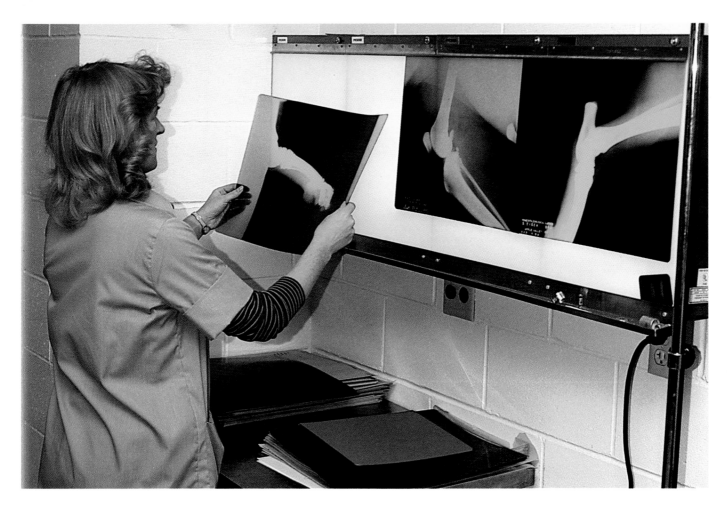

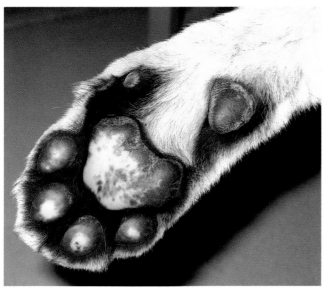

bothering it. X-rays are often taken and are especially helpful for finding problems as with this tiger's injured paw.

Even a tiger that appears perfectly healthy is given a complete physical every year. The yearly physical is much like the physical given upon arrival at the zoo, except that vaccine shots are not given at each and every physical. The yearly physicals and periodic immunizations are continued throughout the tiger's life.

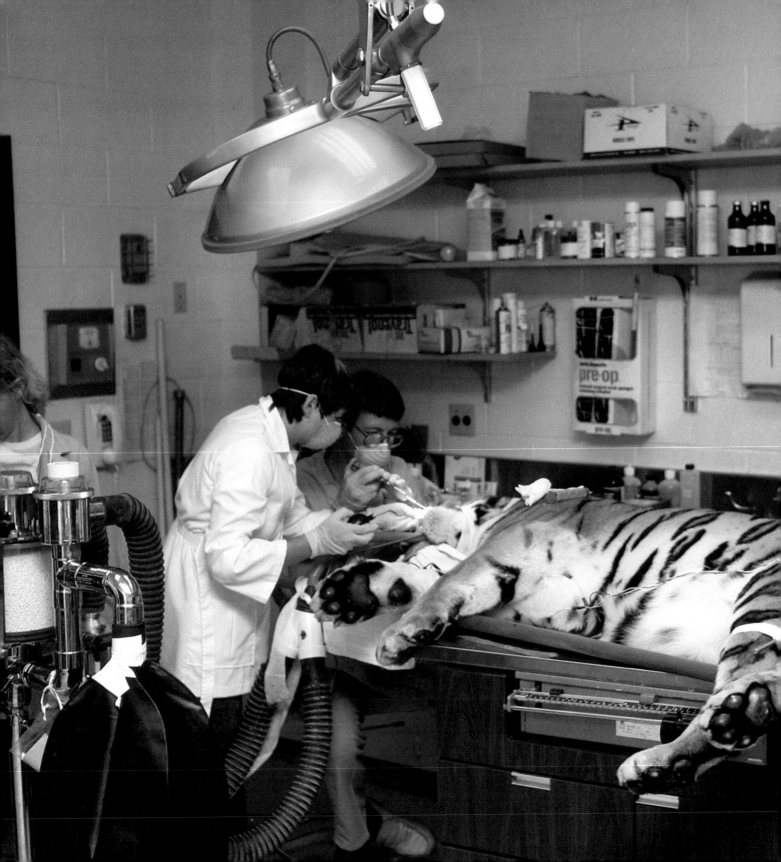

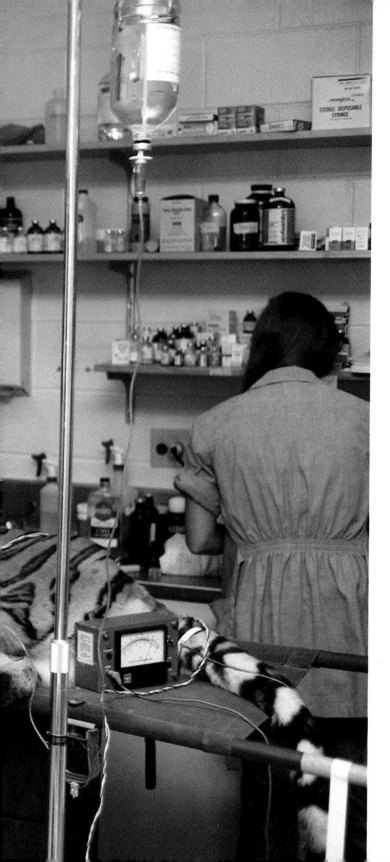

The yearly physical includes a dental check as well. Once a week, the tigers are given bones to chew on. This helps keep their teeth clean and strong. Nevertheless, tigers do sometimes develop dental problems. When a Siberian tiger needs dental work, the zoo vet calls in a dentist, who could be the same dentist that you go to. Except for the fact that they are longer, the tools the dentist uses on the tiger are much the same as those used on people. Of course, the tiger is put to sleep before the dentist begins work! In these pictures the Siberian is receiving root canal work. This is when the root of a tooth is badly infected and has to be removed through a hole drilled into the tooth.

Tigers, both captive and wild, become **sexually mature**, or able to mate and bear young, at the age of three years. A male and female chosen for mating are put next to each other in separate cages. Although the bars of the cages separate them, the tigers can see each other and are close enough that they can pick up the other's scent.

While in these cages, the tigers are watched closely by the zookeepers. If the tigers seem to get along fairly well, they are put together in one cage for mating.

With zoo tigers, the female is the **aggressor**, or one that approaches the male and shows willingness to mate. She will rub up against the male and then

assume a squatting position. The male tiger then mounts her and mating takes place. Right away, the female rolls over and swats the male with her paw. The male must jump away to avoid the sharp blows. After going their separate ways for the next 7 to 10 minutes, the female initiates the whole mating process again.

Female zoo tigers mate only with males specially chosen for them according to genetic backgrounds. The proper combination of genes provides stronger and more stable cubs. This process is called **selective breeding**.

Females usually produce a litter of two or three cubs after a **gestation period** of 90 to 110 days. When ready to give birth, pregnant females are allowed access to an area called the maternity den. There she can give birth to her cubs in peace and quiet. Generally, vets are not present during birth. Females become anxious and defensive during this time and might attack a human "helper." If the female seems to be having severe trouble delivering her cubs, however, the vet will sedate her and perform a **caesarean section**, or deliver the cubs through a cut in the mother tiger's abdomen.

When the cubs arrive, they are kept with their mother in the tiger nursery. Within the first week of the cubs' lives, the mother is removed to an area next to the nursery. Her cubs are then given physicals and begin the first of a series of twice-weekly "weigh-ins." These weighings continue for several months and help zoo vets keep track of the tiger cubs' growth.

For the first 12 weeks of their lives, the cubs **nurse**, or drink their mother's milk. As they get older, they begin to eat meat. Because tigers are fed meat daily, it is difficult for a mother tiger to teach her cubs how to hunt. Sometimes, however, she shakes large pieces of meat in her jaws, just as she would

if she were making a kill in the wild. Occasionally, a mouse or other animal will enter the tiger's area and will fall victim to the tiger's hunting instinct. The mother tiger lets out low growls so other tigers around her—including her cubs—will keep away while she eats. By observing these behaviors, the young cubs learn many of the ways of the wild

tigers from which they have descended. Even in the zoo, the tiger's basic instincts are strong.

It is only the mother tiger, however, that helps bring up the babies. The father tiger will have nothing to do with his offspring.

In the wild, the mortality, or death, rate of Siberian tiger cubs is very high. Probably only one or two cubs from a litter would survive one year. In a zoo, however, two out of three cubs survive. This can sometimes create problems for the zoo. A tigress may have up to seven litters in her lifetime, but a zoo cannot take care of too many tigers at once. If too many tigers are born, the zoo is responsible for finding a place for some of the "extra" tigers at another zoo. If this is not possible, a tiger is occasionally **euthanized**, or put to sleep. This may sound cruel, but it is really often the best way of dealing with the problem. Special zoo committees make decisions concerning these homeless tigers.

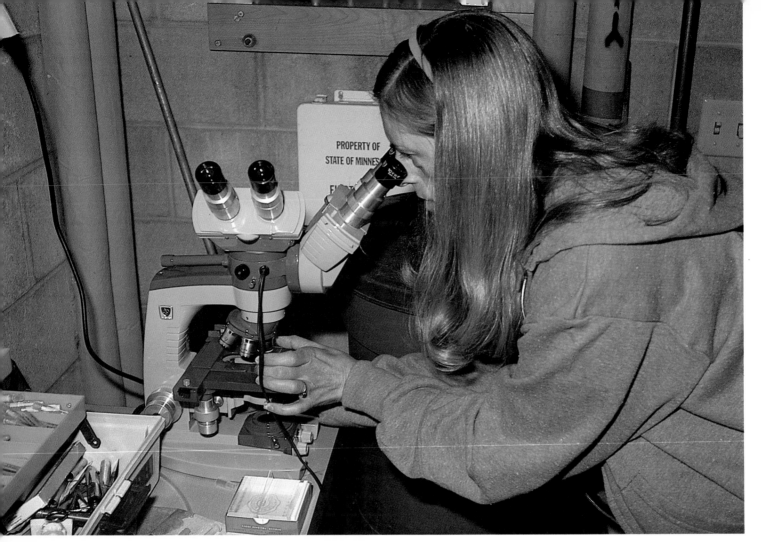

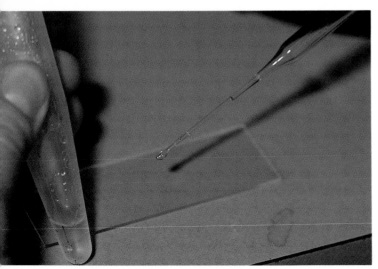

It is also the zoo's responsibility to be selective about breeding so that the tigers that are born have strong bloodlines. At the present time, 85% of the Siberian tigers in the United States are descended from one of three bloodlines. This is a problem. In order for the Siberian tiger to survive and remain a strong species, more variety in genetic makeup must be introduced. One way to do this is through **artificial insemination**. In

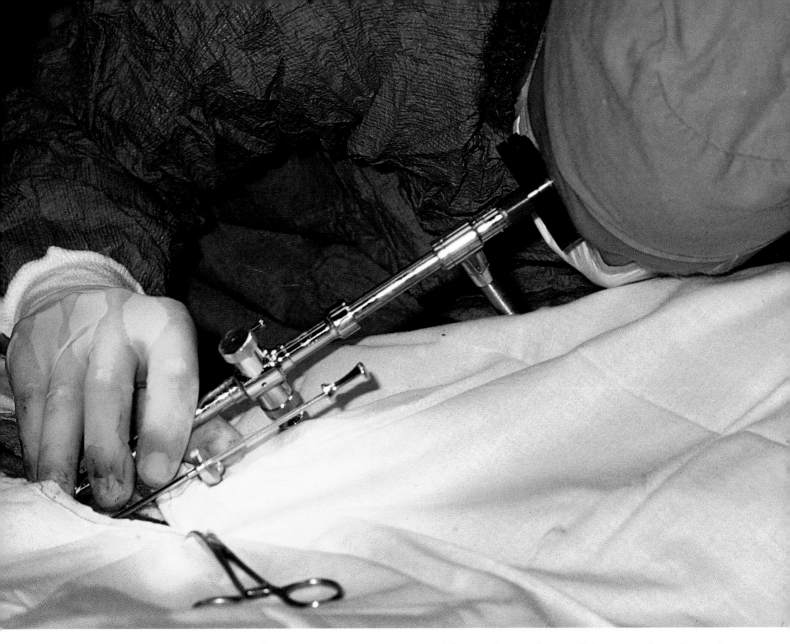

artificial insemination, the sperm, or male reproductive cells, of a male tiger is injected into a female tiger in the hope that a pregnancy will take place. Through artificial insemination, sperm can be taken from male tigers thousands of miles away, even from tigers in the wild, and implanted in captive females, thus strengthening the genetic diversity of cubs without having to import the male tigers. Although artificial insemination of tigers has not been successful so far, there is hope for better results in the near future.

The life span of a Siberian tiger differs according to the conditions in which it lives. A Siberian in the wild may live for up to 12 years if its habitat is not too close to that of human beings, if there is plenty for it to hunt and eat, and if no natural disasters, such as forest fires, occur. Siberians in captivity live for about 20 years, since life in captivity is a good deal easier than life in the wild.

Today only 350 Siberians remain in the wild. This number will probably not increase, since the area in which they now range cannot support additional tigers and it is unlikely that a new wild habitat can be created for them. Through the care and protection of people, however, the 350 can remain a steady number, and many more Siberians can thrive in captivity.

GLOSSARY

caesarian section: an operation in which a baby is born by being taken out of the womb through a surgical cut

cub: a baby tiger

endangered species: a kind of animal that is threatened with extinction

euthanize: to put an animal to death because it is in a hopeless state of health or has nowhere to live safely

extinction: when all the animals of a certain kind, or species, die

gestation: the period of time it takes for a baby to develop before birth

habitat: the area in which an animal normally lives

keeper: a person employed by a zoo to care for the animals

nocturnal: active mostly at night

reserve: land designated for use as a natural-habitat living area for animals, where the animals are protected from hunters

sedative: a drug given to induce a relaxed or sleeping state

territory: an area of land that an animal guards as its own

tigress: a female tiger

vaccine: a substance given to people and animals, usually by innoculation (shot), to prevent disease

veterinarian: a medical doctor who treats animals

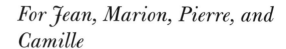

For Jean, Marion, Pierre, and Camille

Copyright © 1998 by Siphano, Montpellier. First American edition 2000 published by Orchard Books
First published in Great Britain in 1998 by Siphano Picture Books UK

Orchard Books, A Grolier Company, 95 Madison Avenue, New York, NY 10016

Manufactured in the United States of America. Printed and bound by Phoenix Color Corp.
Book design by Mina Greenstein. The text of this book is set in 17 point Bulmer MT.
The illustrations are watercolor. 10 9 8 7 6 5 4 3 2 1

Library of Congress Cataloging-in-Publication Data
Bassède, Francine. A day with the Bellyflops / by Francine Bassède.—1st American ed. p. cm.
Summary: On the first day she tries to work in her new office set up in the old toolshed, Mrs. Bellyflop is continually interrupted by the antics of her three children.
ISBN 0-531-30242-3 (trade).—ISBN 0-531-33242-X (lib. bdg. : alk. paper)
[1. Pigs—Fiction. 2. Working mothers—Fiction. 3. Mother and child—Fiction. 4. Brothers and sisters—Fiction.]
I. Title. PZ7.B29285Dat 2000 [E]—dc21 99-27171

A Day with the Bellyflops

Francine Bassède

ORCHARD BOOKS · NEW YORK

*L*illy, Peter, and Wiggly Bellyflop were very proud of Mother's new office in the old toolshed in the garden. They had helped to fix it up, and they had even given Mother their best drawings to hang on the walls.

"I only have two hours of work to do," said Mrs. Bellyflop. "If you play quietly and don't interrupt me, I will be finished soon."

"Afterward, can we make an apple pie?" asked Lilly.

"Why not?" said Mother.

Mrs. Bellyflop made herself comfortable in her office. It still smelled of freshly cut wood and paint.

Lilly slipped on her tutu and danced on the lawn, while Peter put Wiggly on the swing and gently pushed her.

They all looked as pretty as a picture.

Suddenly Lilly appeared at Mother's door with a scowl on her face.
"Peter and Wiggly messed up my tutu.

They are playing with the hose."

"The hose is only for the plants," Mrs. Bellyflop reminded them firmly as she dried Wiggly with a soft towel.

Mrs. Bellyflop had barely started working again when she heard loud footsteps outside the window.

Peter had eaten all the apples they had saved for the apple pie.
"I was hungry," he mumbled, his mouth full of apples.

Mother brought out the cookie tin and sat the children on the grass for a picnic.

But the picnic ended sooner than she expected. She hadn't even sat down when she saw four familiar ears passing by the window.

"What's all this mess?" she asked angrily.

"Wiggly dived into the mud and now there's mud all over us too," grumbled Peter and Lilly.

Mother gave them all a hot, soapy
bath, dried them off, and cleaned Lilly's
tutu and Peter's scooter.

"Now you must promise to play quietly!" said Mother. "I only have two hours of work to do and then we can all play together."

"We promise!" said Peter, Lilly, and Wiggly. They smiled sweetly and smelled very fresh and clean.

Lilly brought out her face paints. "Let's all be clowns," she suggested.

At last, some peace and quiet!

"Let's play circus," said Peter, jumping on Wiggly's tricycle.
"We'll be the acrobats," said Lilly as she and Wiggly took off on
Peter's scooter. "Here we go!"

"Now everybody hop on the scooter. I've seen that in the circus," said Peter.
"YAHOO!" they all cried. "YAHOO!" on the turn, and "YAHOO!" on the slope. Then . . .

SPLASH!
SPLASH!
SPLASH!

Three Bellyflops in the mud!
Mother heard the splashes from her office.

She didn't say anything. She simply grabbed
the hose and turned on the water.

"I thought the hose was for the plants . . . ," Peter
began, but Mother paid no attention. Without
uttering a word, she watered the piglets until
they were back to their bright pink piggy color.

At that moment, Mr. Bellyflop came back from
the market.

"Come and help me cook dinner," he said to the children. "Let's let Mother work."

But Mrs. Bellyflop found all kinds of excuses to stay in the kitchen . . .

just to be sure that things
didn't turn out like the last time
Mr. Bellyflop and the children
did the cooking.

It was late now. Daddy put Lilly, Peter, and Wiggly to bed, while Mother straightened up the house. Then he brought her a cup of tea and said, "You'll be able to work now, my dear."

Mrs. Bellyflop longed to go to bed
herself, but she had to go back to
her new office in the old toolshed
in the garden.

She still had two hours of work to do!